DK READERS

Level 1

Level 2

A Note to Parents

DK READERS is a compelling program for beginning readers, designed in conjunction with leading literacy experts, including Dr. Linda Gambrell, Distinguished Professor of Education at Clemson University. Dr. Gambrell has served as President of the National Reading Conference, the College Reading Association, and the International Reading Association.

Beautiful illustrations and superb full-color photographs combine with engaging, easy-to-read stories to offer a fresh approach to each subject in the series. Each DK READER is guaranteed to capture a child's interest while developing his or her reading skills, general knowledge, and love of reading.

The five levels of DK READERS are aimed at different reading abilities, enabling you to choose the books that are exactly right for your child:

Pre-level 1: Learning to read
Level 1: Beginning to read
Level 2: Beginning to read alone
Level 3: Reading alone
Level 4: Proficient readers

The "normal" age at which a child begins to read can be anywhere from three to eight years old. Adult participation through the lower levels is very helpful for providing encouragement, discussing storylines, and sounding out unfamiliar words.

No matter which level you select, you can be sure that you are helping your child learn to read, then read to learn!

LONDON, NEW YORK, MUNICH,
MELBOURNE, AND DELHI

DK LONDON
Series Editor Deborah Lock
Art Director Martin Wilson
US Editor Shannon Beatty
Production Editor Francesca Wardell
Jacket Designer Martin Wilson

Reading Consultant
Linda Gambrell, Ph.D

DK DELHI
Senior Editor Priyanka Nath
Senior Art Editor Rajnish Kashyap
Assistant Editor Deeksha Saikia
Assistant Designer Dhirendra Singh
DTP Designer Anita Yadav
Picture Researcher Sumedha Chopra
Managing Editor Alka Thakur Hazarika
Managing Art Editor Romi Chakraborty

First American Edition, 2013
Published in the United States by DK Publishing
375 Hudson Street, New York, New York 10014

13 14 15 16 17 10 9 8 7 6 5 4 3 2 1
001—187465—June/2013

A catalog record for this book is available
from the Library of Congress.

ISBN: 978-1-4654-0892-1 (Paperback)
ISBN: 978-1-4654-0893-8 (Hardcover)

DK books are available at special discounts when purchased in bulk for sales
promotions, premiums, fund-raising, or educational use.
For details, contact:
DK Publishing Special Markets
375 Hudson Street, New York, New York 10014
SpecialSales@dk.com

Color reproduction by Colourscan, Singapore
Printed and bound in China by L Rex Printing Co., Ltd.

The publisher would like to thank the following for their kind permission to
reproduce their photographs:

(Key: a-above; b-below/bottom; c-center; f-far; l-left; r-right; t-top)

2 Corbis: Imaginechina (br); Ken Paul / All Canada Photos (tr). **Great Southern
Railway:** (clb). **David Gubler:** (cla). **3 Dreamstime.com:** Tommaso79 (cb). **4-5
SuperStock:** age fotostock (b). **6 Corbis:** Christophe Boisvieux. **7 Dorling
Kindersley:** Rough Guides (tr). **SuperStock:** Xavier Forés / age fotostock (b). **8
Alamy Images:** Matthew Clarke (clb). **8-9 Orient-Express Hotels Trains &
Cruises:** (b). **9 Orient-Express Hotels Trains & Cruises:** (tr). **10-11 Alamy
Images:** Keren Su / China Span (b). **12-13 SuperStock:** Wolfgang Kaehler (b).
13 Alamy Images: Andrew Gransden (cla). **Corbis:** Richard Ross (br). **14-15
Great Southern Railway:** (t). **16 Alamy Images:** JTB Media Creation, Inc. (bl).
17 Alamy Images: Image Gap. **18-19 Getty Images:** Iris Kuerschner / Look (b).
19 Alamy Images: Sonderegger Christof / Prisma Bildagentur AG (t).
Dreamstime.com: Nui7711 (br). **20-21 David Gubler:** (t). **21 seat61.com. 22
Corbis:** Ken Paul / All Canada Photos. **Photoshot:** Mel Longhurst (bl). **23 Alamy
Images:** Jack Sullivan (t). **24-25 Getty Images:** Gavin Hellier / The Image Bank
(b). **25 Corbis:** Michael S. Yamashita (t). **26-27 Getty Images:** Denis Charlet /
AFP (b). **28-29 Dreamstime.com:** Mamahoohooba (b). **29 Corbis:** Imaginechina
(t). **32 Alamy Images:** Matthew Clarke (tl). **Corbis:** Richard Ross (cl). **Dorling
Kindersley:** Rough Guides (clb). **Dreamstime.com:** Nui7711 (cla). **Photoshot:**
Mel Longhurst (bl). **33 Getty Images:** Erich Hafele / age fotostock (br)

Jacket images: *Front:* **Corbis:** Dan Sherwood / Design Pics

All other images © Dorling Kindersley
For further information see: www.dkimages.com

Discover more at
www.dk.com

DK READERS

Train Travel

Written by Deborah Lock

DK Publishing

Tickets please!
Climb aboard!
Watch your step!
We are going on a trip of
a lifetime to see the world by train.

It's a slow start as we wind
our way up a mountain.
We are on a small train in India.
The ride will take eight hours.

Puff!

Puff!

We have picked
up speed.
We are on
a steam train.

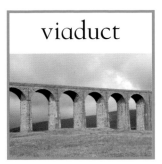

viaduct

We travel from the mountains
to the sea in Scotland.
This viaduct has 21 arches.
It's been standing
for more than 100 years.

Dinner is served!
We are on the famous
Orient Express.
We are traveling from city
to city in Europe.
A diesel engine pulls
the shiny old carriages.

carriages

Whoosh!
We zigzag through
the Andes mountains in Peru.

This track is called
the "Railroad in the Clouds."
It's the second-highest railroad
in the world.

Sit back and relax.
We have a long trip ahead on
the longest railroad in the world.

We are traveling all the way across Russia.

Goods trains pull more than 200,000 containers along this railroad every year.

container

Look out for kangaroos!
We are traveling through

the middle
of Australia.

We are on a very long train
called the Ghan.
It can pull lots of carriages.
It can be nearly a mile
(over a kilometer) long.

Are you tired?

This is the most comfortable

train in the world.

You have your own bedroom

on the Blue Train.

Come and sit in the lounge.

Enjoy the views

of South Africa.

Look! There's a

herd of elephants.

Do you like bridges?
There are about 300 bridges on
this trip through the Swiss Alps.
The windows are huge so
you can see everything.
Click, clack!
The train uses cogwheels
to go up and down steep hills.

cogwheel

This is the Silver Lady.

It has a diesel engine.

It's like a silver thread streaking

through the United States.

At night, you can rest

in the sleeper carriages

or on a chair that leans back.

vistadome

Do you like long trips?
This train takes four days
to travel across Canada.
It goes across prairies, over rivers,
and around lakes.
Sit on the top level.
You'll get the best views from
the vistadome.

Are you in a hurry?
This train in Japan is fast!
It's like a bullet, whizzing
from station to station.
This electric train gets its
power from the wire
above the track.

It's dark!
We are in a tunnel dug in
the rock under the sea.

The sea is between England
and France.
This fast train takes 35 minutes
to go through the long tunnel.

Our trip ends on the fastest
train yet!
Its rails are high above
the ground.
This train in China uses
magnet power.

What trains will you go on
in the future?

Take a look at where
you have been.
Which was your favorite
train trip?

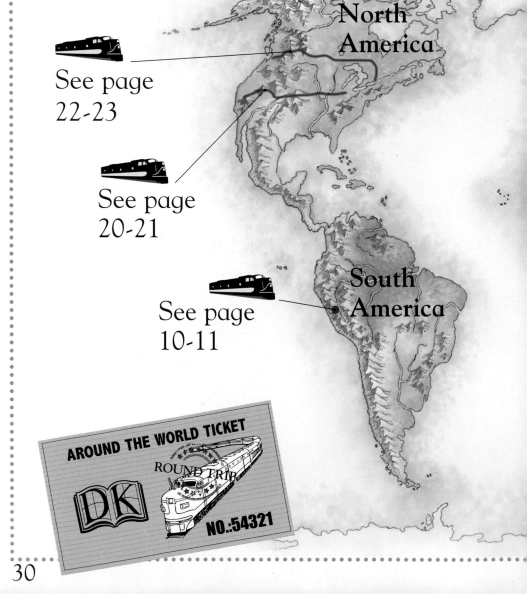

North
America

See page
22-23

See page
20-21

South
America

See page
10-11

AROUND THE WORLD TICKET
ROUND TRIP
DK
NO.:54321

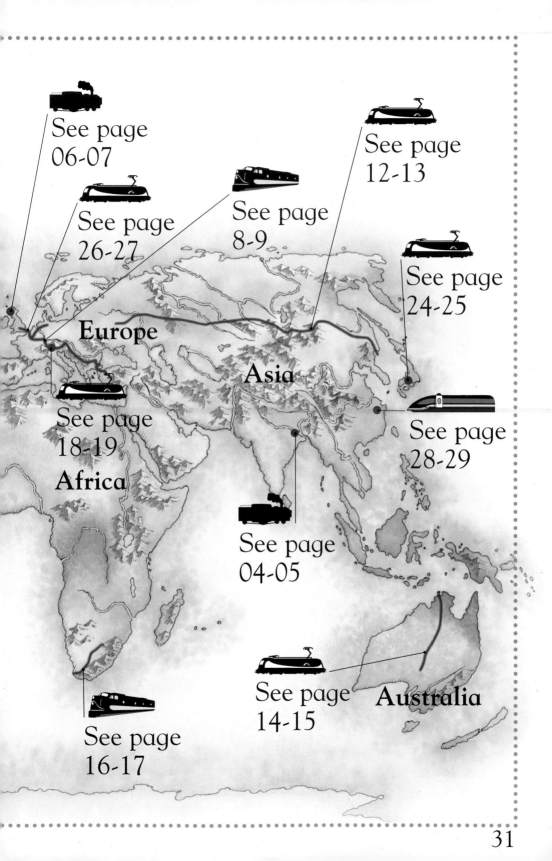

See page
06-07

See page
26-27

See page
8-9

See page
12-13

See page
24-25

Europe

Asia

See page
18-19

Africa

See page
28-29

See page
04-05

See page
14-15

Australia

See page
16-17

Glossary

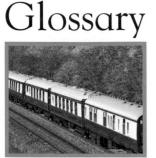

Carriages
wheeled vehicles that carry many people

Cogwheel
a wheel with raised parts called teeth

Container
a large metal box that carries goods

Viaduct
a bridge with arches with a road or rails on top

Vistadome
a carriage with a glass dome on the top